Quickstart Guide to Google AdWords

Jonathan Oxer

Published February 2008 by Lulu Press
© Copyright 2008 Jonathan Oxer
ISBN: 978-1-84799-649-7

Permissions

This book is distributed under a Creative Commons Attribution-Noncommmercial-No Derivative Works 3.0 License. The full text of the license is available online at http://creativecommons.org/licenses/by-nc-nd/3.0/. In summary, the license includes the following terms:

You are free:

 to Share – to copy, distribute and transmit the work

Under the following conditions:

 Attribution. You must attribute the work in the manner specified by the author or licensor (but not in a way that suggests that they endorse you or your use of the work).

 Noncommercial. You may not use this work for commercial purposes.

 No Derivative Works. You may not alter, transform, or build upon this work.

- For any reuse or distribution, you must make clear to others the license terms of this work. The best way to do this is with a link to the web page above.
- Any of the above conditions can be waived if you get permission from the copyright holder.
- Nothing in this license impairs or restricts the author's moral rights.

Disclaimer

This book is sold as is, without warranty of any kind, either express or implied. While every precaution has been taken in the preparation of this book, the author and publisher assume no responsibility for errors or omissions. Neither is any liability assumed for damages resulting from the use of the information or instructions contained herein. It is further stated that the author and publisher are not responsible for any damage or loss to your data or your equipment that results directly or indirectly from your use of this book.

Trademarks

All terms mentioned in this book that are known to be trademarks or service marks have been appropriately capitalized. The author and publisher cannot attest to the accuracy of this information. Use of a term in this book should not be regarded as affecting the validity of any trademark or service mark.

The Big Picture

About This Guide..7
Basic Principles..9
Getting Started...21
Managing Your Account..45
Creating Additional Ads..57
Maximising Performance..61
Understanding Your Bills..69
Additional Resources...73
Glossary..75

What's Inside

About This Guide..7
Basic Principles..9
   What Is The Google AdWords System?.................................9
   Search Network vs Content Network....................................13
   Understanding CPC and CTR..14
   How Google Ranks Ads..15
   Tracking Multiple Campaigns...17
Getting Started...21
   Create Your First Campaign...21
   Select Edition..23
   Customer Targeting..25
   Create Ad..27
   Select Keywords..29
   Pricing Information..31
   Initial Bid Optimisation..35
   Review Your Selections...39
   Sign Up..41
   Submit Payment Information..43
Managing Your Account..45
   Campaign Management..45
      Account Snapshot...45
      Campaign Summary...45
      Tools..46
      Conversion Tracking...46
      Website Optimizer..47
   Reports..49
      Report Center..49
      Create Report..49
   Analytics...51
      Getting Started..51
      Analytics Settings | View Reports.................................52
   My Account..55
      Billing Summary..55
      Billing Preferences..55
      Access...55
      Account Preferences..55
Creating Additional Ads..57
   Campaigns, Ad Groups, and Ads..57
      Campaigns...57
      Ad Groups...57

  Ads..58
  Creating A New Campaign...58
  Creating Ad Groups..59
  Creating Ads...59
Maximising Performance...61
  Finding Good Keywords..61
    Initial Keyword List..61
    Broaden Your List..61
    Set Match Type..62
  Creating Landing Pages..64
  Search Network vs Content Network..65
Understanding Your Bills..69
  Billing Frequency..69
  Credit Limits...69
  Billing Summary Adjustments...70
Additional Resources...73
  Ultimate Guide To Google AdWords...73
  AdWords For Dummies..73
  How To Build A Website And Stay Sane......................................73
  Inside AdWords Blog..73
Glossary..75
  Ad...75
  Ad Group...75
  Campaign...75
  Click Through...75
  Click Through Rate (CTR)...75
  Conversion...75
  Conversion Rate..75
  Cost Per Click (CPC)..76
  Cost Per Thousand (CPM)..76
  Destination URL..76
  Display URL..76
  Impression..76
  Keyword...76
  Landing Page...77
  Local Targeting..77
  PageRank...77
  Pay Per Click (PPC)...77
  Placement Targeting...77
  Quality Score...77
  Search Engine Optimization (SEO)...77

Linux Support Australia
Expert Commercial **Linux** support
Onsite or Remote (**Australia**-wide).
www.cybersource.com.au

www.OnWorld.com.

Enjoy Australia's la
of X10/A10 **home**
www.envioustechr

AdWords Ma
Free Quotes Si
SmartClix.com

Vacuum Cleaner Auction
Bid On Wide Range of Top Brand
Vacuum Cleaners From $9 at Grays.
www.graysonline.com.au

Save on a **bagless vacuum**,
Get 30-80% off on our huge range!
DealsDirect.com.au

Paying $1
Adwords Str
Expensive Cl

Automation Engineering
Systems Integrator - 6 Locations in
Victoria NSW NZ. Rockwell, Citect
www.Integrated**Automation**.com.au
Victoria

Connected Living
Custom installation specialists in
Audio Visual and
www.connectedlivir
Victoria

Home Automation Made Easy
Wireless modular system
Retrofit your existing **home**
www.tec**home**.com.au

Maui Molokini Snorkel
Hot Deal: $59.95 Morning Molokini
and Turtle Town snork
www.**maui**-vacation.n

Ducted Vacuum - Australia
Installed or DIY Free Call
Australia wide - Ph 1800 333 222

AdwordsStrategy.c

Scuba Diving - Oahu
Beginner & Certified **Scuba** Tours
Off of Waikiki, Hawaii - $94.99
www.HonuHawaiiActivities.com

About This Guide

This quickstart guide will walk you through the process of getting started with AdWords, showing you how to promote your business online without confusing you with jargon or over-complicating things. It will show you the basics of how to get started, how to create and tune your ads, and how to measure the effectiveness of your ads. It assumes no technical knowledge: just a desire to grow your business and an interest in how AdWords can help bring new customers to your site.

To get the greatest benefit from this guide please treat it as a series of hands-on exercises. Follow the steps to sign up for an AdWords account if you haven't done so already and try things out for yourself. Effective use of AdWords is a constant learning process so don't stop once you have your first ad campaign up and running: keep testing and experimenting with different ads to get the best possible return on investment for your advertising dollars.

Once you've worked through this guide there are a huge number of more advanced resources that you can use to develop more sophisticated AdWords campaigns, so at the end of this guide I'll refer you to the ones that I think are the best.

Good luck!

scuba training in maui - Google Search - Mozilla Firefox

File Edit View History Bookmarks Tools Help

http://www.google.com.au/search?q=scuba+training+in+mau | cuba training in maui

Web Images Maps News Video Gmail more ▼   jonoxer@gmail.com | My Notebooks | Web History | My Account | Sign out

Google scuba training in maui   Search   Advanced Search / Preferences
Search: ⦿ the web ○ pages from Australia

Web   Results **1 - 10** of about **23,500** for **scuba training in maui**. (0.21 seconds)

Maui Scuba Schools: PADI Diving Classes, Courses & Lessons
Maui Scuba Schools; offering PADI Home Study **Scuba** Diving Classes, Courses & Lessons on **Maui**. Begin your studies at home, finish on **Maui**.
www.mauiscubaschools.com/ - 20k - Cached - Similar pages - Note this

Yahoo! Directory AU & NZ > **Scuba Training** and Instruction
Scuba training and certification agency. Red Sea **Scuba** Diving College Open site in a new window ... Offers **SCUBA** certification and diving tours of **Maui**. ...
au.dir.yahoo.com/Business_and_Economy/Shopping_and_Services/Outdoors/**Scuba**/**Training**_and_Instruction/ - 34k - Cached - Similar pages - Note this

Maui SCUBA Diving Certification, courses, **training**, classes ...
Snorkeling on **Maui** with **Maui** Diving Snorkel shop/**maui** diving **scuba** center, on **Maui**, Hawaii. Daily BOAT **scuba**, snorkel trips and rentals.
www.mauidiving.com/booking.html - 25k - Cached - Similar pages - Note this

Maui Scuba Diving with Lahaina Divers: **Scuba** Dive **Training** and ...
Lahaina Divers is **Maui's** favorite **scuba** diving shop. Plan your Hawaii dive vacation with us and you'll find the best boat diving, **scuba** instruction, ...
www.lahainadivers.com/**scuba_training**.html - 40k - Cached - Similar pages - Note this

  Lahaina Divers - Handicapped **Scuba Training**
  Maui Handicapped **Scuba** Diving • Dive Tours and Dive **Training** Maui Scuba Dive Charters • **Scuba** Certification • **Scuba** Gear Rentals

Sponsored Links

Scuba Diving Melbourne
Learn **Scuba** Free Mask,Snorkel,Boots
Shop Online Now, Large Range
www.aquability.com.au
Victoria

Maui Scuba Diving
Pride of **Maui** Offers Exclusive
Scuba Diving Tours to Molokini.
www.prideofmaui.com

Maui Molokini Snorkel
Hot Deal: $59.95 Morning Molokini
and Turtle Town snorkel tour
www.maui-vacation.net

Scuba Diving - Oahu
Beginner & Certified **Scuba** Tours
Off of Waikiki, Hawaii - $94.99
www.HonuHawaiiActivities.com

Single **Scuba** Divers

Done

Basic Principles

What Is The Google AdWords System?

When a user goes to www.google.com and performs a search, the Google system does two different things at the same time. Firstly it searches through its list of known websites to find sites that are most relevant to the user's nominated keywords and displays them in a list on the left side of the results page. However, while that is happening it also matches those same keywords against Google's list of active AdWords ads, finds ads that match the user's keywords, performs some other calculations and then displays the best matches in a list on the right side of the results page. The results page therefore contains a combination of organic results on the left and paid results on the right.

For example, a search for "scuba training in maui" will result in a list of sites on the left that match those keywords but also a list of paid results on the right, with the paid results matched up to the user's search terms in order to provide advertising that is likely to be relevant to what they are looking for at the time.

Because the paid results are formatted in a very simple way and appear quite similar to organic results many people don't even notice the difference.

It's a simple concept but also incredibly powerful, because the ads in the paid results don't need to be widely broadcast to a large audience in the hope that some of those people may be interested. They can be targeted to appear only when users search for very specific terms, resulting in ads that are very relevant to that particular user at that particular moment and therefore extremely effective. And you, the advertiser, can run as many different ads as you like all with individual targeting based on keywords, user location, and other factors – and you can change and tune your ads and targeting parameters live online at any time, based on the statistics and results that Google report on the performance of your ads.

Many website owners spend a lot of time modifying and tuning their site to achieve the best possible results in the organic search listings on the left. This process is known as Search Engine Optimization, or SEO, and is covered in numerous books and online guides. There is also a whole industry of SEO consultants who can help you tune your site for the best possible organic search result position.

But what most website owners fail to take advantage of are the paid results on the right. Getting your site listed in the paid results on the right is easy: all you need to do is set up an AdWords account, create an ad, specify your keywords, and pay Google to display it.

It's a marketer's dream come true.

AdWords ads can also appear on third-party websites, reaching people not just when they are searching but also when they are browsing the web generally. And it doesn't take much to get started: even a budget of a few dollars per day is enough to get your ad campaign underway and start bringing people to your site. You can specify a budget when you set up your AdWords account and know you'll never spend more than you can afford.

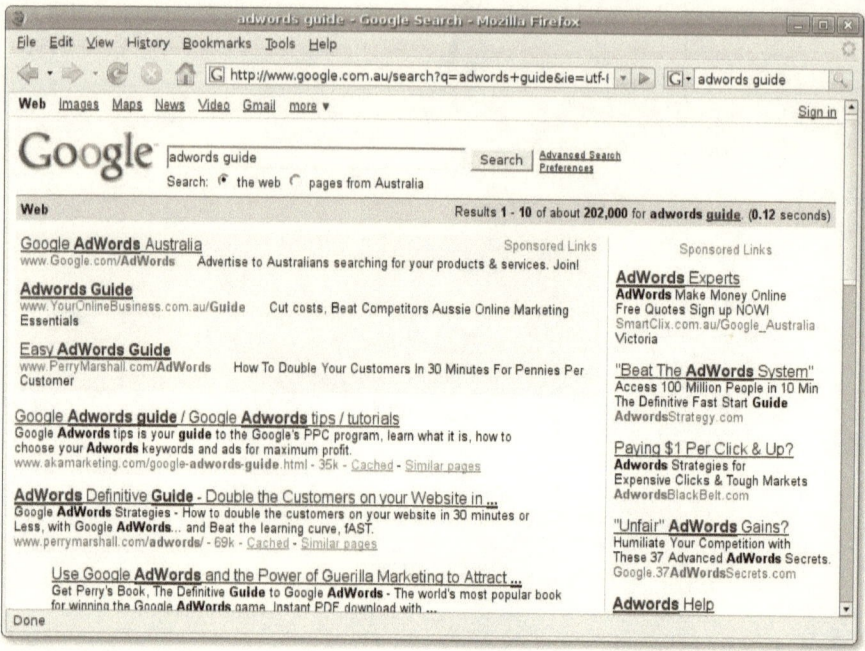

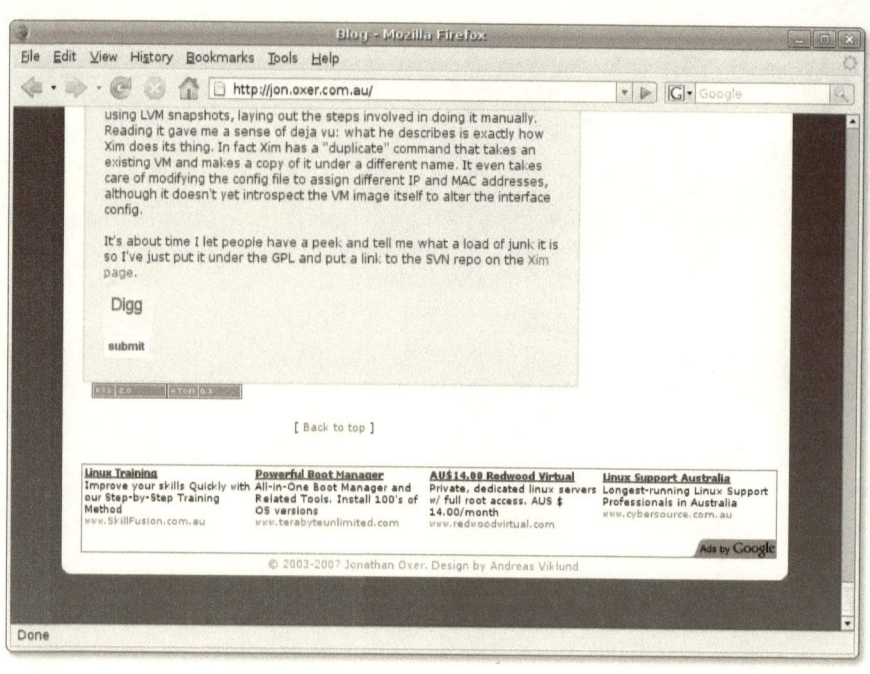

Search Network vs Content Network

AdWords ads can appear in two quite different places: the search network and the content network. The search and content networks are fundamentally different so it's important that you understand what they are.

The term "search network" refers to places where Google search results are displayed, most commonly the Google search engine itself but also some other sites that display the Google search form. Paid AdWords ads relevant to the user's search terms are displayed down the right hand column like in the first screenshot on the left, where the paid ads are selected based on relevance to the user's search keywords.

The term "content network" refers to third-party websites that display AdWords ads in order to gain a share of the advertising revenue paid to Google by advertisers. AdWords ads displayed in the content network can appear anywhere on the page, like in the second screenshot on the left where they appear at the bottom of my personal blog. The ads in this example are related to Linux because the AdWords system has picked up on that as a keyword in the content of some of my blog posts, so it selects ads that are most likely to be relevant to readers of my blog.

For now the critical thing is that you understand that there are two different types of location where your ads can be displayed. We'll return to this concept later to discuss the differences in mindset between users on the two networks and how to optimise your ads for one network or the other.

Understanding CPC and CTR

Two terms that you'll encounter a lot as you create and manage your ads are "CPC" and "CTR".

CPC is an abbreviation for Cost Per Click. It's the amount you pay to Google each time a user clicks on one of your ads. If your ad is displayed but not clicked, you don't pay a thing: it's only if your ad is clicked that Google will charge you a fee. So you're not simply buying a fixed number of ad placements like with traditional media. What you're paying for is the number of potential customers who actually respond to your ad by clicking on it. Obviously the higher your CPC the more you'll be paying for each potential customer, so your goal is to have a low CPC.

CTR is a closely related term, and it's an abbreviation for Click-Through Rate. It's the percentage of people who see your ad and then click on it, so it's a critical indicator of the performance of an ad and the accuracy of your targeting. For example, if your ad is displayed 100 times and 4 people click on it, that gives you a CTR of 4%. A high CTR means that your ad is both well written and also targeted at the correct audience. On the other hand, a good ad can be undermined by poor targeting and vice versa. Your goal is to have the highest CTR possible.

How Google Ranks Ads

Now that you understand keyword targeting, cost per click, and click through rate, it's time to put those concepts together and see how Google decides the order in which to display ads.

The specific algorithm used is a closely guarded secret, but the end result is that a number of factors all influence how highly your ad will rank so it's important to cover all the bases.

The first major factor is keyword targeting. Google have been incredibly successful in the search market because they are extremely good at matching up keywords to web pages and finding the most relevant matches, and the same principles apply to ads. Getting your ad keyword targeting correct is critical.

The second factor is the cost per click that you are willing to pay. The AdWords system is actually a big auction mechanism: if multiple advertisers want their ads to appear for the same keywords, the advertiser who is willing to pay more will have their ad appear higher in the listing more often. It's a free-market system so some highly-contested keywords require a very high CPC bid to get your ad to appear at all, while more specific or obscure keywords may go for only a few cents. It's all about market pressure.

The third factor is your click through rate. When your ad starts there is no historical data about how well it performs so Google applies an average value initially, but once your ad has been displayed a number of times your CTR is calculated and factored into the ad ranking algorithm. Ads that perform well are rewarded with higher rankings, while poorly performing ads may drop right down or be deactivated entirely.

The fourth factor is the quality of your actual website. This is an issue that many AdWords first-timers overlook, and for the first few years of the AdWords system it didn't seem to have much (if any) influence on ad ranking. However, in mid 2006 an update to the AdWords ranking algorithm had a cataclysmic effect for many advertisers as they saw their required CPC bid make a huge jump: in some cases it went from a few cents to US$5 per click, which is enough to make many lead generation campaigns unviable. That event has come to be known as the "Google slap", and involved the addition of site quality factors to the ad ranking system. The sites that were hardest hit were micro-sites set up just for Google ads and didn't have much content. As a result you now need to spend at least a little bit of time optimizing your site for search engines and obtaining the highest possible "PageRank" score for your site if you want your ads to rank well and pay a lower CPC.

All those factors and more are factored into your ad ranking.

Therefore your objective should be to target your keywords carefully, minimise your ad spend by bidding a cost per click value that's just high enough to get your ad into a good position, maximise your ad performance by tuning it to get the highest possible click through rate, and tune your website for a good PageRank score. There's no single magic bullet: you can't just rely on paying large CPC fees alone, or good PageRank. You need to cover all the bases.

A lot of this guide will focus on explaining how to do exactly that, but above all else there is one critical point you need to keep in the back of your mind at all times: think like a customer. Don't obsess over algorithms and statistics to the extent that you forget about the real people who will read your ads. Put yourself in their shoes and think about what is important to them, what they're searching for, what problems they are trying to solve – and therefore how you can be relevant to them.

As my friend and Search Engine Optimization expert Chris Burgess likes to say, "think like a searcher". The correct mindset will help your advertising campaign far more than a big budget.

Tracking Multiple Campaigns

If you want your AdWords marketing budget to be effective one of the most important principles to understand is ad segmentation and tracking. With traditional marketing media such as letterbox drops it is very difficult to measure effectiveness at all, let alone for specific geographic areas or demographics: you need to do things like create special promotional codes and make a record of all the responses, and the results can then take a long time to collate.

A Google AdWords program, on the other hand, allows you to run as many different campaigns at once as you like and provides incredibly fine-grained tracking of results for each ad variation. This is a vital performance tuning tool because it means you can run multiple ads against each other with only minor differences between them and compare the results to find out which is the most effective. It's a bit Darwinian: put multiple ads up against each other and see which one wins, then dump the loser, make another ad that's a variation on the winner and repeat the process all over again, continually striving for the best possible result. The law of the AdWords jungle is survival of the most successful.

As a general principle it's best to run separate ads for each customer segmentation profile and ad content variant so you can compare results between them. For example, instead of running a single campaign with global distribution you should run separate campaigns for each country or even region so you can see which performs best. And instead of putting all your keywords into one ad, create a different ad for every keyword and compare the results.

You will find many places in the Google AdWords management interface where you can select multiple options for a particular setting such as target region. In my opinion you should deliberately blind yourself to the fact that those settings let you select multiple options: treat every single multi-entry setting as if you are only allowed to choose one thing, not several.

If you are entering an option such as target country and you're tempted to add in a second country, don't! It's better to over-segment your AdWords program by creating a separate ad for every option you want to select, even if everything else about the ads is identical.

Yes, you may end up with dozens or even hundreds of slightly different ads by doing it this way, but if you get into good habits like this right from the start you'll thank me eventually because a highly segmented campaign methodology will give you tremendous insight into individual ad performance.

In this guide we'll start by creating just one very specifically targeted ad and then later we'll go through the process of creating additional ads, ad groups, and ad campaigns that can be tracked and managed independently.

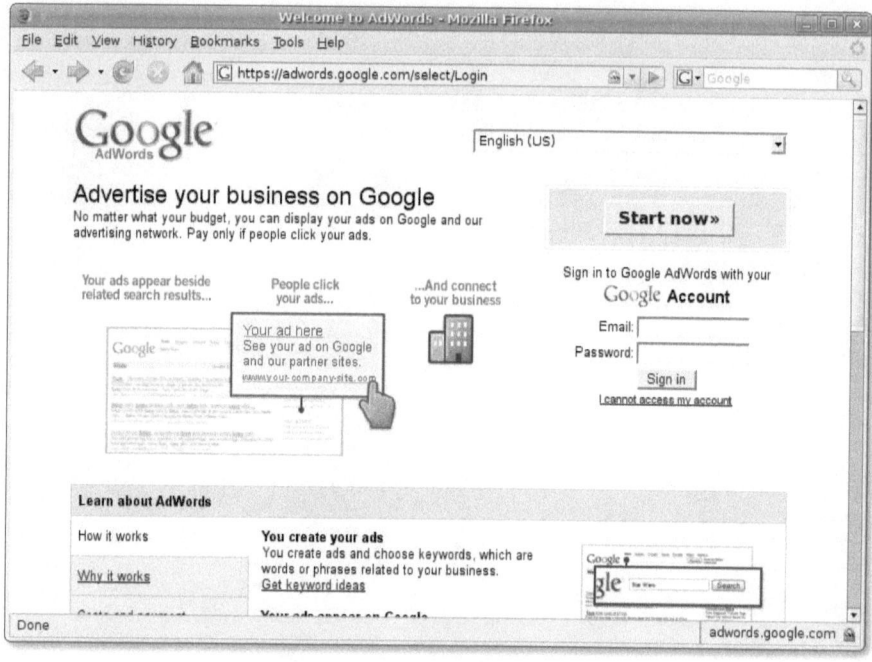

Getting Started

Create Your First Campaign

Start by pointing your browser at https://adwords.google.com to get to the initial setup page. This page provides some introductory information about the AdWords program and also includes links to helpful resources such as Frequently Asked Questions and even live online chat with Google staff if you need personal assistance.

If you have previously used AdWords you can sign in on this page and get right into it, but if you don't have an account yet don't worry: just click the big "Start Now »" button to get the process underway.

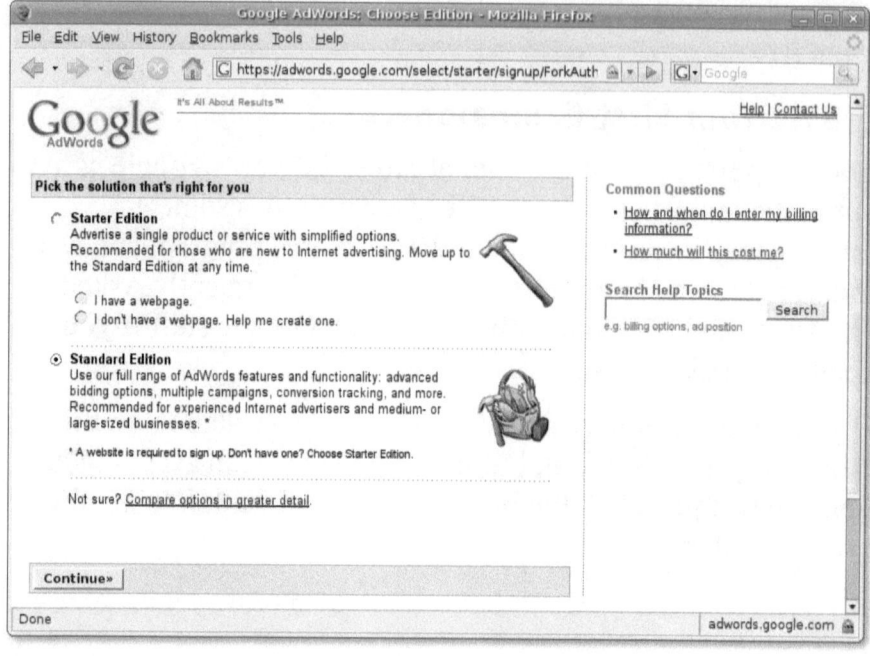

Select Edition

Google provide two different "editions" of AdWords: Starter Edition and Standard Edition.

Starter Edition is designed to simplify a couple of aspects of account management with a streamlined signup process and by presenting you with a limited number of options, while Standard Edition gives you full access to all features. There is no other difference between the editions and the costs are exactly the same: you can even begin with the Starter Edition and upgrade it to Standard Edition at any time.

However, I recommend that you begin with the Standard Edition right away. Don't bother with the Starter Edition because it limits you to one product and a single set of keywords; provides only basic campaign activity reporting; limits your customer targeting options; doesn't provide you with access to the traffic estimator tool; forces you to set your spending limits by month instead of by day; and prevents you performing site-specific location targeting.

All of those are very useful features when it comes to optimizing your ad performance, so go for the Standard Edition right from the start to get maximum benefit from your ad campaigns.

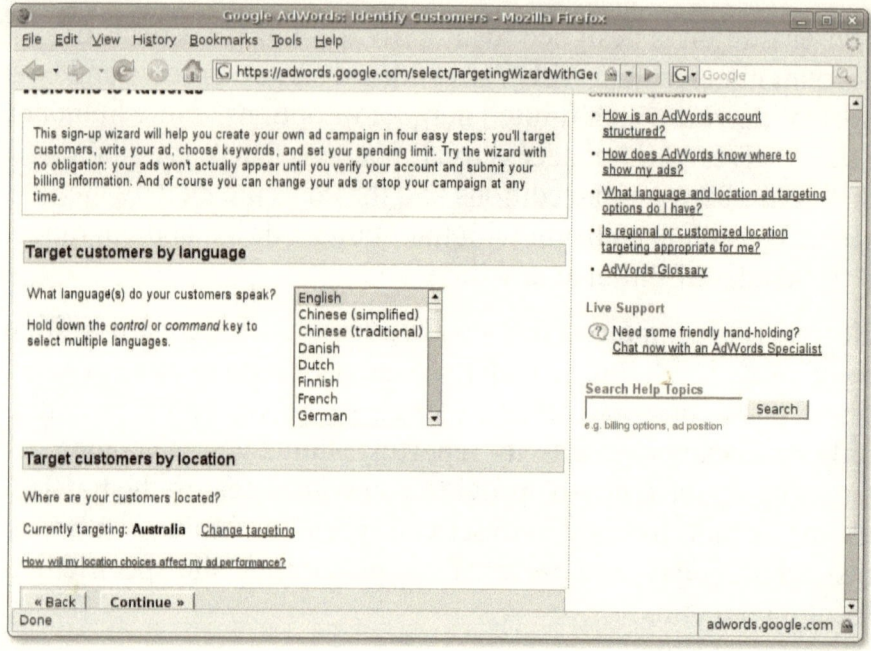

Customer Targeting

The very first thing to specify when setting up your first ad campaign is your target language and location.

Although you can select multiple target languages for an ad it's best to stick to just one language per ad.

Obviously your ad needs to be written so that it can be read by customers in your selected target language. In some unusual situations it may make sense to write your ad in one language and target another: for example, many people can read English as a second language and perhaps you want to reach native German speakers who can also speak English, so you may decide to write your ad in English but set the ad target language to German.

However, when targeting multiple languages it's better to set up separate campaigns for each language anyway so you can track their performance individually.

Location is also a critical factor. Once again my preference is to keep each ad campaign laser-focused on a specific target audience and then run multiple campaigns to reach different audiences, so select a single region or country for your first campaign.

Click the "Continue »" button when you're happy with your selections.

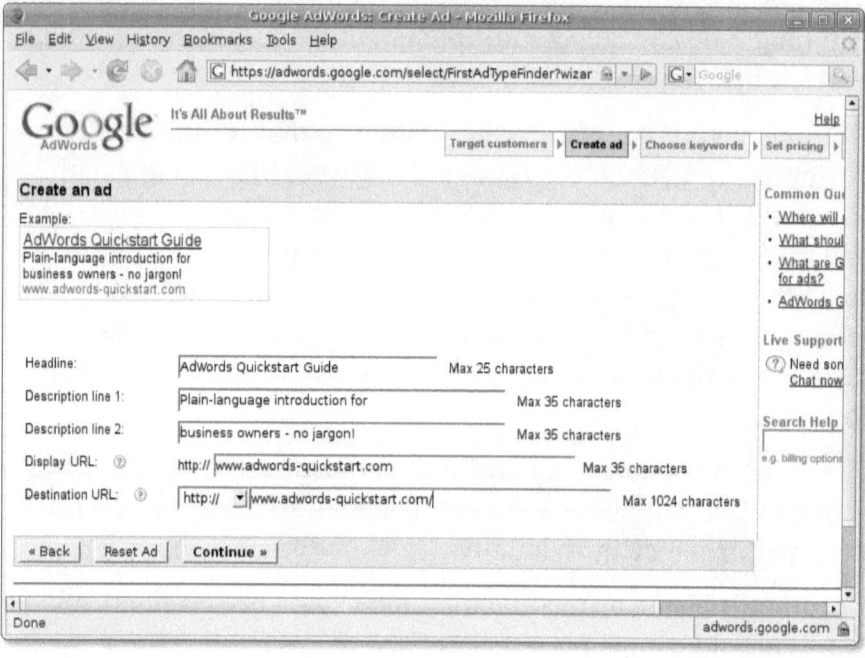

Create Ad

Now it's time to create your first ad. There are very tight restrictions on how AdWords ads can be structured, so you must make your ad fit within the following criteria:

Headline (maximum 25 characters)

Description line 1 (maximum 35 characters)

Description line 2 (maximum 35 characters)

Display URL (maximum 35 characters)

Destination URL (maximum 1024 characters)

Not much space to play with!

The tight restrictions on AdWords ads can feel like a curse when you first try working within them, but it's actually a blessing in disguise: the terse nature of the ads is what makes them so effective and it forces you to carefully think through and optimize your marketing message. You can't afford to waste a single character so it's critical that every word is part of the message you want to get across.

Note the difference between "display URL" and "destination URL". Because ad space is very limited you can only have up to 35 characters displayed in your URL, but when a user clicks on your ad they will actually go to the destination URL. This is great for performance tracking and tuning because it means you can display a common URL for all your ads, but have a different "landing page" for each ad so users will arrive at a page that is tuned to be relevant to that specific ad.

We'll cover landing pages in detail later and you'll have plenty of opportunity to tweak your ad after it starts running, so do the best you can for now but don't spend hours agonising over it. Optimization is best done with hard data rather than guesswork so once you have an ad that you're happy with as a starting point click "Continue »" at the bottom of the page to move on.

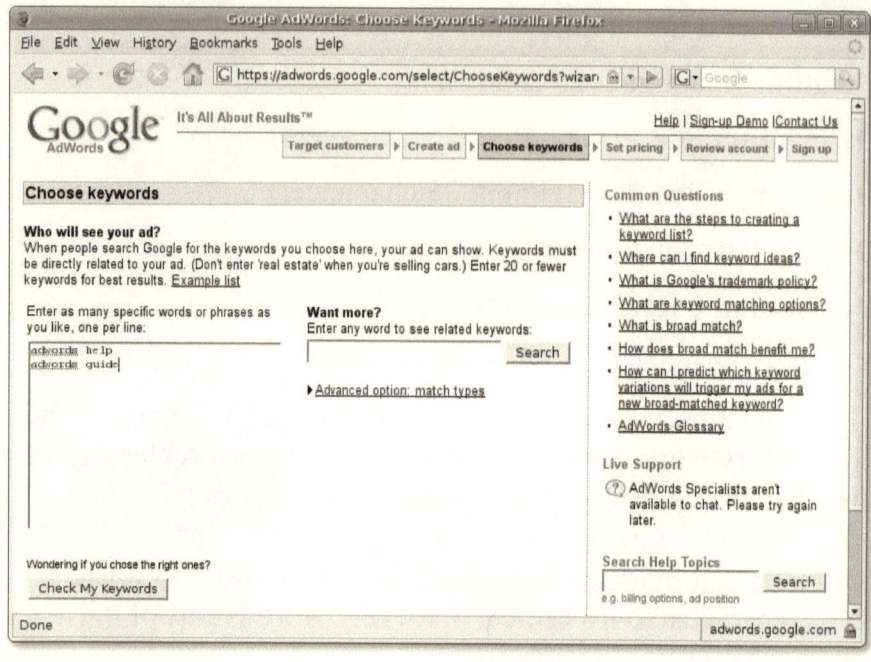

Select Keywords

AdWords ads are only displayed when the keywords associated with that ad match a user's search terms (on the search network) or page keywords (on the content network) so keyword selection is your opportunity to specify who should see your ad.

For your first ad it's best to stick to keywords that are directly related to the product or service you are promoting. In a moment we'll be specifying that we only want this ad to appear on the search network, not the content network, so keep in mind that people who see the ad will be very focused on solving a particular problem or answering a specific question. If your ad isn't relevant to their problem it's not likely to achieve a good click-through rate.

Although you could enter a big list of keywords at this point I recommend that you don't: stick to just a single entry so you know that your ad will only be displayed for that specific keyword or phrase. Later you'll be able to create multiple ads for different keywords so that you can track and compare the results independently.

Once you have entered your desired keywords for this ad, click the "Check My Keywords" button under your keyword entry box to have Google run a quick sanity-check on it. If all goes well it will simply tell you that all your keywords checked out OK. If not, follow the instructions to make your keywords meet Google's criteria.

When that's all done click the "Continue »" button at the bottom of the page.

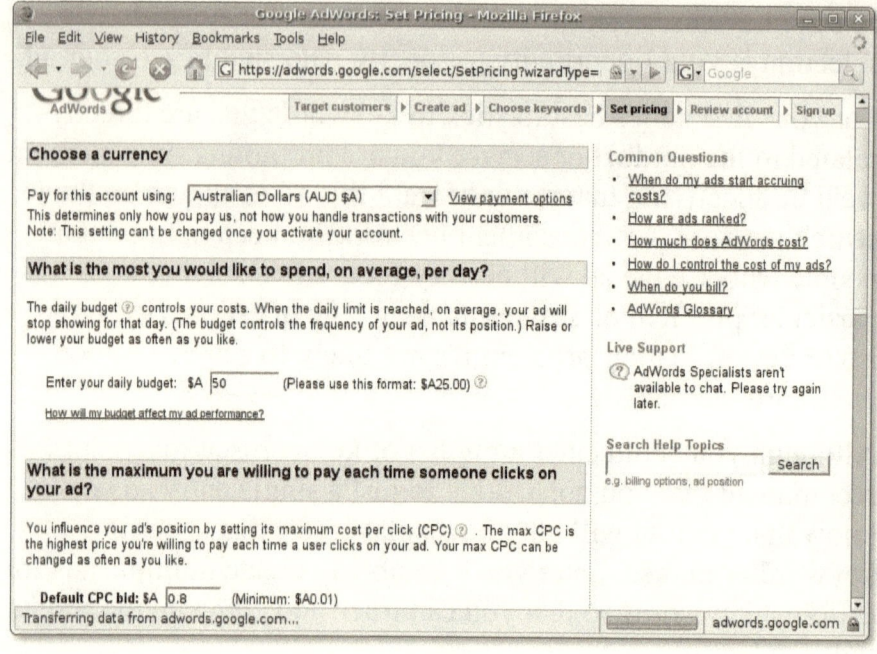

Pricing Information

Next you will be taken to a screen where you can set your preferred currency and pricing information for your ads. One of the most powerful aspects of Google AdWords is that it allows you to adjust your ad parameters on the fly so these are just starting values: in a moment we'll take a look at how to go about tuning and managing your ads to get the best possible performance.

The first option allows you to select the currency that you will use to pay Google for your ads. This has nothing to do with how you sell your products to your customers: it's purely so that Google knows what currency to use when billing you. For example you could be an Australian company selling to American clients in US$, but it may be more convenient for you to receive your AdWords invoices in AU$ for accounting purposes.

Overall there are two immediate factors under your direct control that determine how often your ad is displayed and how high up the rankings it appears: your spending limit and your ad bid. Understanding these two factors is crucial to running an effective ad campaign.

Your spending limit is simply the most that you want to spend in total per day on your campaign: it's the total budget that you want to allocate. Once your daily spending limit has been reached your ad will stop appearing until the next day, preventing you running up large advertising expenses without realising it. It's a bit like a pricing cap on a mobile phone plan: a safety net to ensure you don't blow all your money in one go. You can start low and adjust it later if you like, so set an appropriate value for your daily budget in the second option.

Rather than just running your ads at every possible opportunity until your budget has been used up, Google uses your daily spending limit as a guide to determine how often to show your ads throughout the day. That way if you run a campaign with a $10 daily budget you won't blow your entire budget in the first 5 minutes each day – appearance of your ads will be spread throughout the day.

The third section of this page is probably the single most confusing decision that a first-time AdWords advertiser has to make, so take a moment to look at the "Default CPC bid" and "CPC Content bid" options and make sure you understand how they work.

As explained earlier, "CPC" refers to cost per click, which is the amount that you pay to Google each time a user clicks on your ad. The "Default CPC bid" setting is the highest value that you want to pay each time someone clicks on your ad when it is displayed on the search network.

Selecting a value for your CPC bid is a bit of a balancing act, and this is where experience and result measurement will allow you to tune your ad parameters to improve their cost-effectiveness over time. If you bid too little, other advertisers going after the same keywords may outbid you and so your ad will tend to appear low down the list of ads and also appear less often. If you bid too high you'll probably be at the top of the ad listings, but you'll be paying more than necessary for your ads and you won't be able to afford to have your ad displayed as often for the same budget. Finding that fine line where you're paying just enough but no more is the holy grail of AdWords bid optimisation!

If you think about how the daily budget and CPC bid values relate to each other it should be fairly obvious that they combine to control how often your ads appear each day. If you have a daily budget of $20 and set a CPC bid of $0.50 your ad can be clicked 40 times in one day before you hit your spending limit: the same budget with a $2 CPC would only allow 10 clicks in one day. Increasing your daily budget or decreasing your CPC bid will allow your ads to run more frequently, and vice versa.

Previously we talked about the difference between the search network and the content network. The "Default CPC bid" value that you just set controls your bid for the search network, while the next option, "CPC Content bid", controls your bid on the content network.

Leave the "CPC Content bid" value empty for now so that this particular ad won't be displayed on the content network at all: you could run your ad on both the search network and the content network simultaneously, but that's generally a bad idea because it means you can't track the results or tune the ad for the different networks. It's much better to create another ad just for the content network so you can see statistics for them independently. We'll get to that shortly.

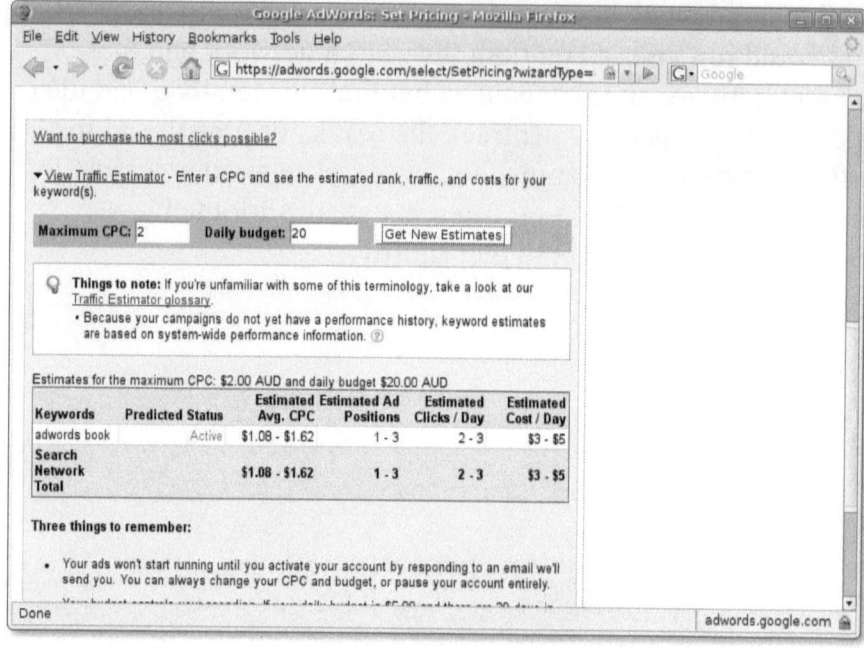

Initial Bid Optimisation

Once you've set your currency, daily budget, and default CPC values you can use the two little helpers at the bottom of the page to get an indication of how well your ad is likely to perform. You'll be able to do a better job of optimisation later when you have actual ad performance data to analyse, but for now these tools will give you some initial estimates based on data from similar ads already in the AdWords system.

The first link, labelled "Want to purchase the most clicks possible?" will show you Google's estimate of the CPC bid you would need to place in order for your ad to win first place in the ad listings every single time. You don't need to bid that much to have a successful campaign, but it gives you a good idea of how competitive those particular keywords are likely to be.

The second link, labelled "View Traffic Estimator", uses the data you've entered to perform a dry-run of your ad campaign and predict its likely performance. This is a very useful tool so make sure you spend a bit of time experimenting with it before you go on. The various columns in the report are:

Keywords: the keywords you have selected for this ad.

Predicted Status: Whether your ad will be active for those particular keywords or not. This is a "threshold" indicator: if it says "Inactive" it means that your CPC bid is so low or your ad quality score is so poor that you will be outbid on every single ad placement and your ads will never be displayed – obviously not a very useful campaign! If it says "Active" it means your ad will appear for those particular keywords.

Estimated Avg. CPC: The amount that you will probably pay per click, which will vary depending on bids by other advertisers.

Estimated Ad Positions: Ads are placed in range blocks, so this column shows which range your ads will be likely to appear in. "1-3" means your ad will appear within the first 3 ads shown; "4-6" means from 4th to 6th position; and so on. Obviously the ideal position is to be as close to the top as possible.

Estimated Clicks / Day: Google's prediction of how many people will click on your ad each day based on the number of times it is shown, the position in the list of ads, and other factors such as performance of other ads bidding for the same keywords.

Estimated Cost / Day: Google's prediction of how much you'll end up spending per day. This may well be lower than your specified daily budget simply because your ad can't be displayed often enough at the nominated cost per click bid to use up your entire budget. There are only a finite number of ad placements available, and Google won't display your ad when your specified criteria such as keywords and CPC bid can't be met.

So play around with the "Maximum CPC" and "Daily budget" values, clicking "Get New Estimates" each time to see how your changes alter the projected result until you're happy with the figures. Note that this is still just a starting point: once your ad campaign is up and running you can fine-tune it until the cows come home.

Once you're ready to move on just click the "Continue »" button at the bottom of the page.

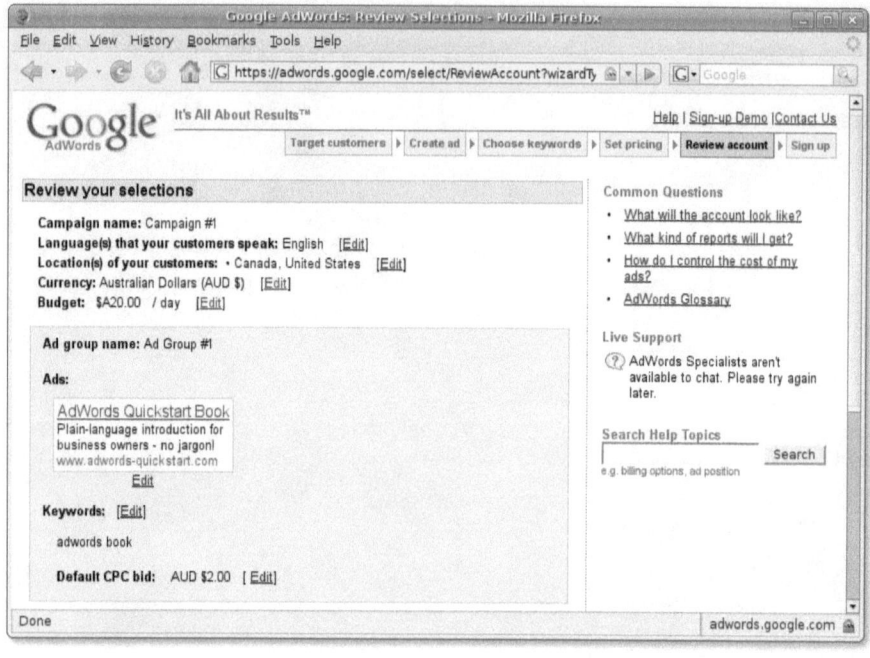

Review Your Selections

Next you will see a "Review your selections" page which summarizes everything you've entered so far and gives you the option of going back and changing your selections. Once you're happy with your selections go down the page and decide whether you want to receive regular emails from Google about AdWords. The first option is to receive personalized ideas for improving ad performance: I recommend you leave this selected so that the Google system can send you automated emails based on its regular analysis of your campaigns. The second option is for their general AdWords newsletter which isn't personalised but can still contain some useful hints and tips.

Once you're done click "Continue to Sign Up »" to move on.

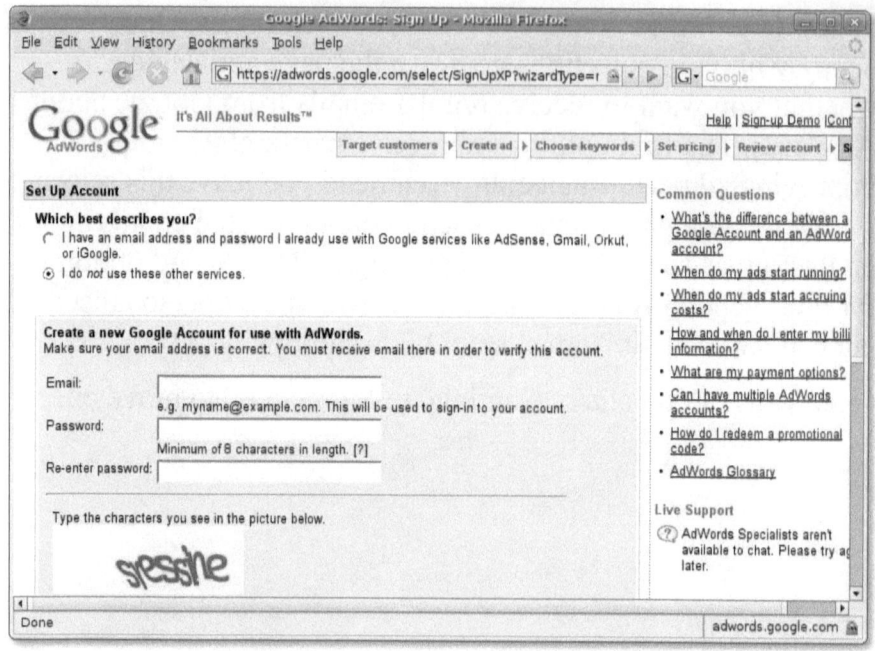

Sign Up

Up until this point you haven't even been required to create an account or sign in, but the next page gives you the option of either using an existing Google-related account such as a Gmail account or creating a new account if you haven't used any Google services before.

Follow the appropriate prompts to select an existing account or create a new Google account, then click "Sign in to your AdWords account" to arrive at the AdWords control panel.

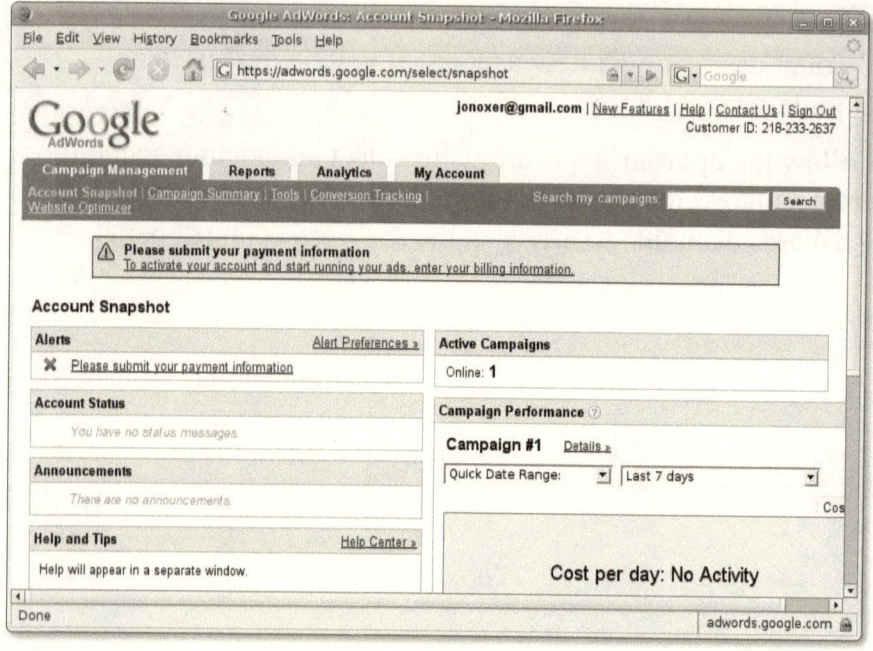

Submit Payment Information

You are now logged into the AdWords management interface, but before your ad campaign can start you need to provide Google with information about how you will pay for your ad placement fees. Click the link under "Please submit your payment information" and follow the prompts to set your location, submit your billing preferences, and specify your payment method.

Google provide two possible payment methods: credit card and bank transfer.

If you choose to pay by credit card you can pay using either postpay billing, whereby your card is charged after your ads have been shown, or prepay billing, where you prepay a specified amount up front and charges are incrementally deducted from that balance.

If you don't have a company credit card available you may prefer the bank transfer option. However, bank transfer cannot be done as postpay billing after your ads have been shown: bank transfer payments require prepay billing to establish a starting credit before your ad campaign can start.

When setting up your account for the first time you will be charged a $10 activation fee.

Submit your preferred payment method to return to the AdWords control panel.

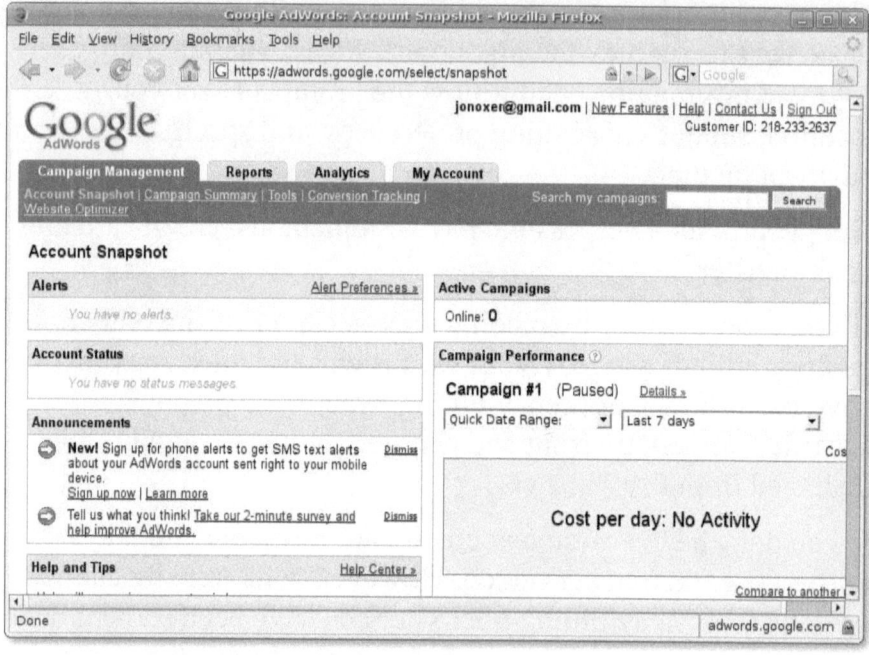

Managing Your Account

When you are logged into the AdWords control panel there are four main sections you can access.

Campaign Management

The Campaign Management area is where you create and manage ads, ad groups, and campaigns.

Account Snapshot

The Account Snapshot section provides you with a dashboard overview of aggregated statistics about all your ads, your billing information, and your alerts: from here you can see how effectively your overall ad budget is being spent and then drill down into specific campaigns for details.

Campaign Summary

In a brilliant piece of creative labelling, the Campaign Summary section provides – you guessed it – a summary of your campaigns! Each campaign is listed with details including the name, status, budget, clicks accumulated, ad impressions, click-through rate, average cost per click, and total cost.

Keep in mind that although the campaign stats are updated frequently, they're not actually real-time. It may take up to three hours for recent activity to appear in the management interface.

One thing that's definitely worth doing is going into the Campaign Summary section, clicking into a campaign, clicking into an ad group, and clicking the "Keywords" tab near the top right of the list. Then click "Customize columns" at the top center of the list to access a drop-down list of columns, and select "Show Quality Score". This will add the Quality Score column to all your keyword reports: a critical indicator of whether Google thinks your ads are good, and therefore how highly they will be ranked.

Tools

The Tools section is basically a list of quick links to a smorgasboard of systems to help you manage your ads. Once you have your first ads up and running it's worth taking some time to go through this section thoroughly and explore all the options, but highlights that many people seem to overlook include:

Site Exclusion. Ads that run on the content network can appear on any one of literally millions of third party websites, and you may decide that you don't want your ads to be associated with a particular company or organisation so the Site Exclusion tool allows you to blacklist specific sites so your ads will never appear on them.

Traffic Estimator. See what the Google system thinks of new keywords before you try them out for real.

My Change History. You had a brainwave and decided to change your ads around expecting them to perform better, but the changes were a flop and you want to change your ads back. No problem – if you remember what changes you made! The My Change History section is like a searchable time machine for your ad campaigns.

Download AdWords Editor. Although you can manage your AdWords campaigns with nothing but a web browser, Google also provide management software that you can download and run directly on Windows or Macintosh computer. The AdWords Editor lets you make bulk changes to ads even while offline, and then apply your changes all in one go next time you connect.

Conversion Tracking

The Conversion Tracking section walks you through the process of setting up conversion tracking for your ads: see which ads are actually providing the biggest payoff for your business. To enable conversion tracking you'll need to be able to make minor changes to your website. If you can't make the changes yourself you may need to have your web developer help you, but it's definitely worth it for the extra information you'll receive about your ad performance.

Website Optimizer

Google have recently made available a pre-release beta of a new tool called Website Optimizer, a system that works with Google Analytics to measure the performance impact of changes to your site. Once Google Analytics is set up on your site you can use Website Optimizer to set up what it calls "experiments": trials of site changes with measured outcomes.

Website Optimizer currently supports two types of experiments.

A/B Split Testing. Create two different versions of a page such as the landing page for your ads and run them simultaneously, with some visitors sent to one page and some to the other. Website Optimizer then keeps track of which version of the page each visitor is sent to and correlates it with your ad campaign, showing you which version of the page works best.

Multivariate Testing. A more complex experiment that involves multiple changes and allows you to track the effectiveness of each change independently.

Website Optimizer is ideally suited to tuning the landing pages for your AdWords campaigns so it's definitely worth a look once you have your campaigns up and running.

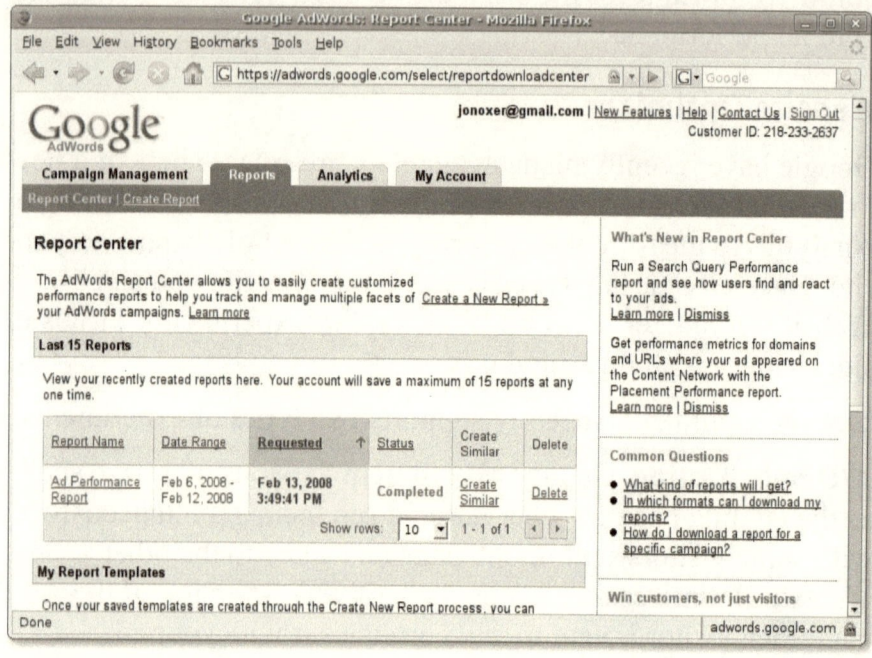

Reports

As you develop an ever-growing collection of ads it will become more and more difficult to keep track of which ones are working well and which should be retired. The Reports section allows you to define and run reports with specific criteria such as ads that contain a specific keyword or ad impressions within a certain date range.

Report Center

See a list of previously generated reports. You can sort by the list columns such as report name and report date simply by clicking the column heading.

Create Report

Generate a new report with your selected criteria by selecting from the options in sections 1 to 3.

Section 4 provides some very useful additional options such as the ability to define a report as a template. If there is a particular combination of factors that you want to analyse regularly a report template can save you a lot of time by allowing you to just select the template next time you come back. You can also choose to have a report regenerated automatically, and even have it emailed to you on completion.

Reports can take some time to run so you may need to create a report and then come back to the Report Center later to view it.

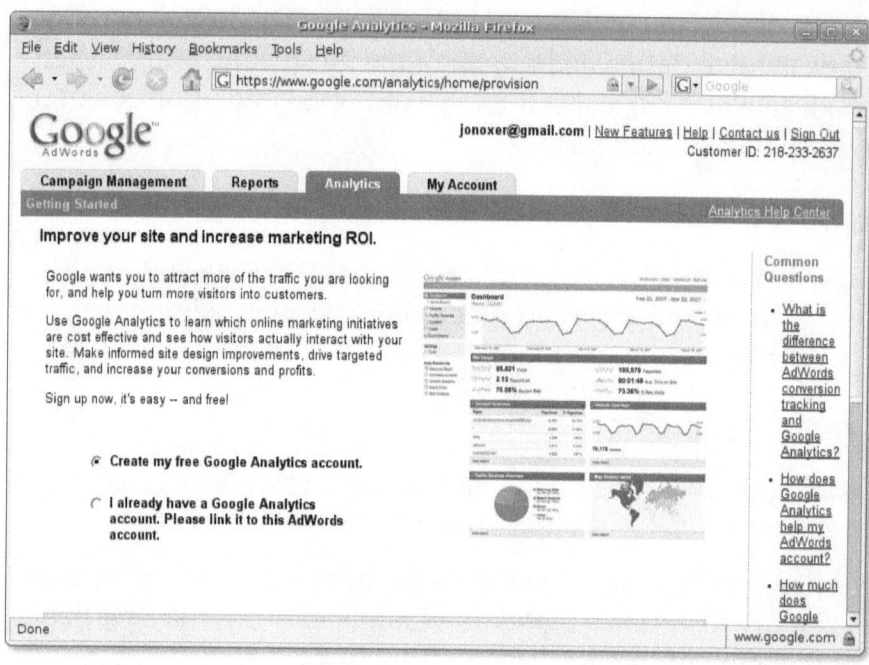

Analytics

Much of your work in optimizing your advertising campaigns will be about comparing what appear to be tiny differences in numbers such as the ad click-through rate, but something to keep in mind is that apparently trivial differences between small numbers can be very deceiving. It can be disheartening to make changes to an ad expecting to see huge results only to see the CTR go from 3.2% to 4.5% because at first glance that doesn't seem like a significant boost, but it is: going from 3.2% CTR to 4.5% is actually a massive performance improvement of 40%! That is, at a CTR of 4.5% you would receive 40% more visitors to your site than you would at 3.2% for the same number of times the ad is displayed.

Google AdWords has excellent internal tools for tracking ad performance metrics such as click-through rate with a great deal of accuracy and you should definitely pay close attention to it. That's not the whole story though: sending people to your site is just the beginning, and tracking what they do on your site is just as important as tracking how they got there.

Google have a very powerful website performance analysis tool called Google Analytics. It's typically used by website owners to track which pages are most popular, which countries your visitors are located in, and how they arrived at the site.

Although AdWords and Analytics are provided as independent Google services, you can link an AdWords account and an Analytics account together to provide very detailed reporting for visitor activity starting with ad display and following all the way through visiting your site, viewing various pages, and performing specific desired actions such as placing an order or submitting an inquiry form.

Getting Started

Go to the Analytics tab in your AdWords management interface to link it to a new or existing Analytics account. By default there will be only a single menu option available: "Getting Started".

Select the appropriate option to create a new account or link to an existing account and click "Continue »" to proceed.

New Account. If you opted to create a new account you will be taken through a series of questions about your website and then you will be shown a simple snippet of tracking code that you will need to add to each page of the site. Adding the tracking code is not particularly difficult and the setup process walks you through exactly what you need to do so if you created your site yourself you should be able to manage Analytics setup, but otherwise you may need to create the Analytics account and then ask your web developer for assistance with the final step of adding the tracking code.

Existing Account. To link your AdWords account to an existing Analytics account you will simply be asked to select the account and log into it if necessary.

Analytics Settings | View Reports

Once you have created a new Analytics account or linked an existing one to your AdWords account the menu options will change and you will see two new menus: "Analytics Settings" and "View Reports". You will then be able to view your Analytics reports directly within your AdWords management interface.

Inside Analytics you will also see a menu option under "Traffic Sources" called "AdWords". From there you can track visitors sent to your site from your AdWords campaigns. However, be aware that Analytics data is only processed every 24 hours and so it may take some time before there is anything to see in the reports.

Using Google Analytics is a big topic in itself so there isn't space to go into all the options and reports here, but one thing you should definitely take the time to set up are your conversion goals.

A "conversion" is when a site visitor performs some action that achieves your business objectives. The click-through rate (CTR) of your ads is important, but that's just the start: you don't advertise just to get people to click on your ads. That doesn't achieve anything! Your ultimate objective is to have visitors perform some action such as placing an online order, or submitting an inquiry form, or subscribing to your newsletter.

Think about what you want people to do after they click on your ad and arrive at your site: that is your conversion goal.

By telling Analytics what your conversion goals are it can then correlate them back to your AdWords campaigns and show you which campaigns result in the best conversion rate.

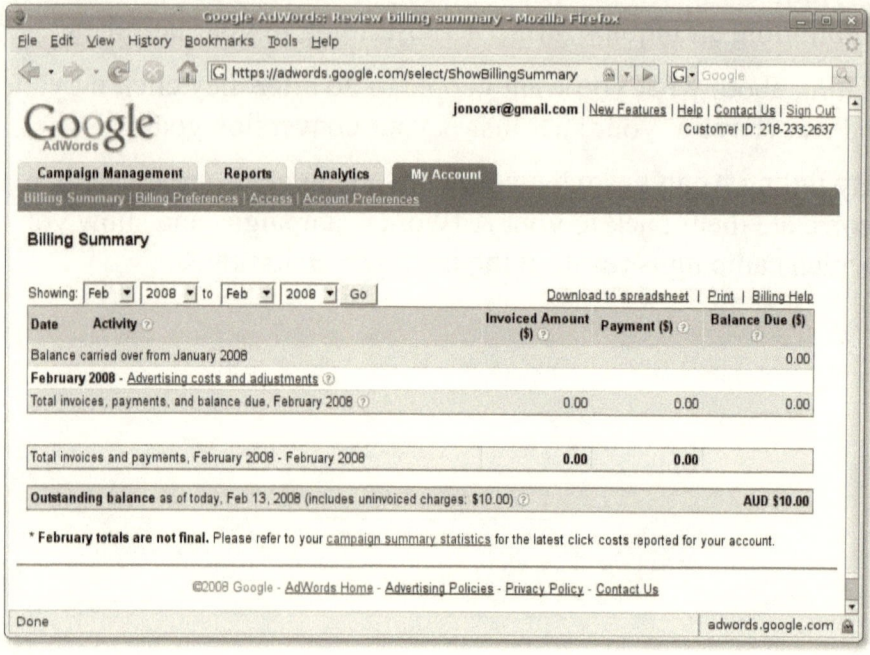

My Account

You can access your past and present billing information online in the My Account section, including details of all adjustments that have been applied.

Billing Summary

An overview of all billing periods and your current outstanding (billed and unbilled) balance. Use the drop-down options at the top of the list to find bills within specific date ranges. You can also download your billing data as a CSV (comma separated values) file that you can open in a spreadsheet such as OpenOffice.org or Microsoft Excel.

Billing Preferences

Set your billing method (postpay or prepay), and bank account or credit card details. This is also where you can redeem coupon codes for special offers that Google may provide: just go to Billing Preferences and enter the coupon code in the "Promotional Codes" section.

Access

If you are running an extensive campaign you may need to allow other users to log into the management interface: the Access section lets you invite other users into your AdWords account so you can collaborate on campaign management. This is particularly useful if you have multiple staff working on a campaign simultaneously or one staff member goes away on leave and another needs to manage their campaigns in their absence. It's far better to allow multiple people to log in with their own accounts than to share a single username and password around.

Account Preferences

The Account Preferences section is a bit of a grab-bag of miscellaneous settings: all the random meta-configuration data is found here, including your account email address; notification preferences; language settings; timezone (useful for getting your report time periods to match your local time); and an AdWords account cancellation form.

Creating Additional Ads

Campaigns, Ad Groups, and Ads

The AdWords system is specifically designed to allow you to run a large number of ads at once, tracking them all independently and structuring them into easily managed groups. This is done using a three-tier system of campaigns, ad groups, and ads.

Campaigns

A campaign is the highest-level grouping available: the thousand-foot view of your advertising program. You can set your advertising budget at the campaign level but not below, so the budget you assign to a campaign is shared by all ad groups within it. At the campaign level you can define:

- The start and end date of each campaign
- The total budget allocated
- Whether to spread ads evenly throughout the day
- Whether to show ads on the search and/or content networks
- Target language
- Target location

If you want to test variations in any of those settings you will need to create additional campaigns and run them in parallel.

Ad Groups

Inside each campaign you can create multiple ad groups. Ad groups inherit all the settings from the campaign they are created in, so settings such as the target language and start/end date that you specify for a campaign automatically apply to all ad groups within it.

At the ad group level you can define:

- Keyword associations
- CPC bid price

Those settings are then applied to all ads within the ad group and cannot be varied, so if you want to test ads using different keywords you will need to create a separate ad group for each set of keywords.

All ad groups within a campaign share the budget allocated to the campaign itself.

Ads

An ad is the smallest unit into which you can divide your advertising program. Ads define the way they will appear to users and the URL they will go to when the ad is clicked, but everything else is inherited from either the ad group or the campaign. The only settings you can change within an ad are:

- Headline
- Description line 1
- Description line 2
- Display URL
- Destination URL

Creating A New Campaign

Go into Campaign Management > Campaign Summary. At the top right of the campaign list are links to create a new campaign. The meaning of the link titles isn't immediately obvious, but they relate to the search network and the content network. To create a new campaign to appear on the search network (ie: next to Google search results) select "keyword-targeted". To create a new campaign to appear on the content network (ie: on third-party websites with matching keywords in their content) select "placement-targeted".

You will then be prompted for a name for your new campaign, so select something that will make it easy to distinguish this campaign in the campaign list.

Because all campaigns must include at least one ad group you will also need to specify the name of the first group in this campaign.

Next you will be prompted to define the first ad in this ad group. This process should be familiar now from when you signed up and created your first ad, so just repeat the steps of creating your ad, defining the targeting, and setting your budget and bid price.

Creating Ad Groups

To create a new ad group first go into Campaign Management > Campaign Summary, then click the name of the campaign where you want to insert the ad group. You can then simply click the "Create new ad group" link at the top left of the ad group list. Once again you'll be walked through the process of specifying the ad group name, then defining the first ad to place within that ad group. You can't create an ad group without also creating an ad to go within it.

Creating Ads

Ads can only be created from within an ad group, so go into Campaign Management > Campaign Summary, select a campaign, then select an ad group. You'll see a summary view with statistics about this ad group and three tabs on the right called "Summary", "Keywords", and "Ad Variations". Select the Ad Variations tab to see a list of all ads within this ad group. Click the link titled "Create an ad variation" at the bottom left of the list to go to a screen where you can enter the details of your ad. To make things easy the screen will be pre-populated with the values from the first ad in the ad group so that you can then simply tweak it as necessary and save the new ad.

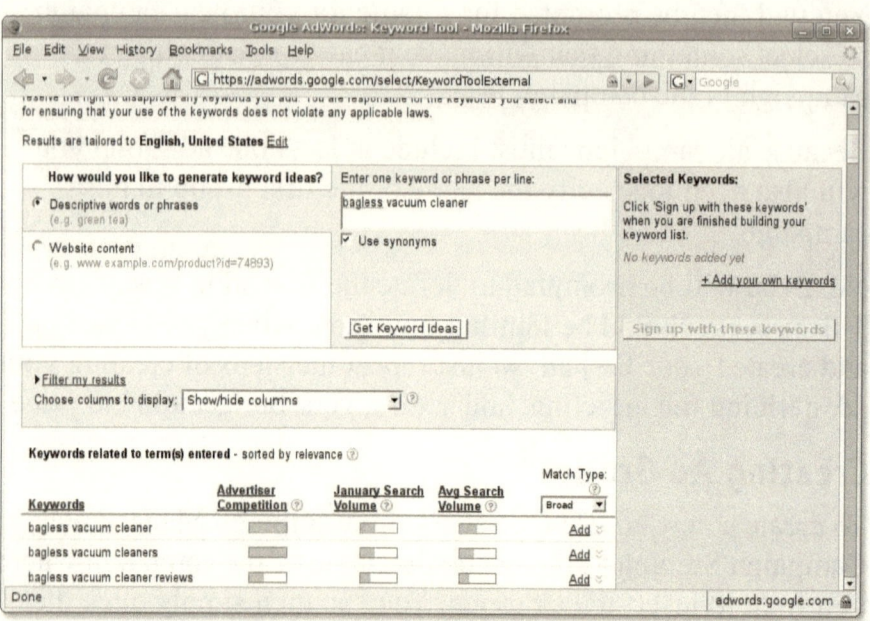

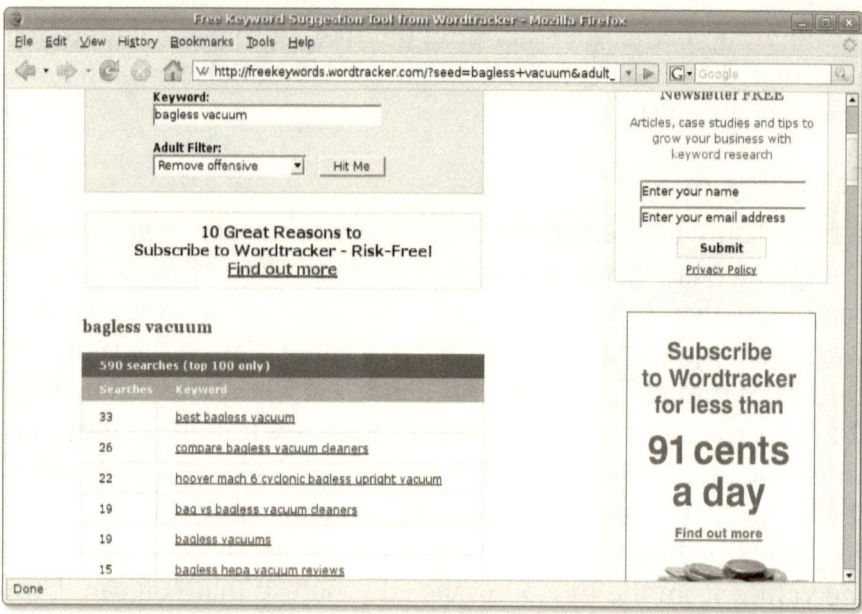

Maximising Performance

Finding Good Keywords

The most important targeting method for your ads is keyword selection: defining which particular words or phrases you want your ads to be associated with.

Initial Keyword List

Start by putting yourself in your customers' shoes. This isn't always easy, because you already know all the jargon and terminology relevant to your particular industry. You need to imagine you're a potential customer who doesn't necessarily even know what words to use to describe what you want. Think back to conversations you have with your customers when they first make contact with you. How do they describe their problem or what they're looking for? Do they use slang words or generic terms to refer to particular products? For example, if you sell vacuum cleaners you may refer to a particular model as "cyclonic" – but maybe your customers will search for "bagless".

So begin by brainstorming a list of keywords as a starting point, putting them all down in a spreadsheet or even just a text document for reference.

Broaden Your List

Now that you have a starting list of keywords it's time to expand it as broadly as possible. The old fashioned dictionary plus thesaurus approach is a great way to come up with words you may not have thought of. And to save you walking over to your bookshelf they're even online now:

http://dictionary.reference.com

http://thesaurus.reference.com

There are also quite a few online tools to help you find related keywords. Google themselves provide one which integrates data from their search engine statistics to report how popular each keyword is. The generated keyword list has relative ratings for how highly contested each keyword is, how often it was searched for last month, and how often it was searched for over the last 12 months:

https://adwords.google.com/select/KeywordToolExternal

Try putting all your brainstormed keywords into the Google tool and see what suggestions come out of it, then add the ones you like to your spreadsheet.

One important thing to note is keywords you see in the list that are not related to your business, but that people may search on when looking for other things. You may find you need to specifically exclude any searches involving those keywords because they're just not relevant to you. We'll get to that in a moment when we set the match type.

Another great online tool is from Wordtracker. Put your starting keywords in and click "Hit Me" to see a list of associated keywords and phrases. You can then simply click any of those phrases to re-seed the tool with that phrase, letting you explore word associations quickly and easily:

http://freekeywords.wordtracker.com

After playing around with these tools for a while you should have quite a list of keywords to work with.

Set Match Type

Now that you have a list of keywords you need to think about how you want them to relate to searches performed by users. For each keyword you have four options: broad match, phrase match, exact match, or negative match.

Broad Match. This is how keywords are treated by default.

With this setting any searches that use that keyword in any order will match your ad, so for example an ad with the keyword "bagless vacuum" will match for any search that includes the word "bagless" and the word "vacuum", such as "bagless vacuum cleaner".

Phrase Match. This setting restricts the match slightly by only matching searches with the words in that exact order and no other words between them. For example, an ad with the keyword "bagless vacuum" would be a phrase match for a search for "cyclonic bagless vacuum", but would not be a match for "bagless cyclonic vacuum".

Exact Match. Setting the exact match option tightens your keywords up even more by requiring searches to be exactly the same as your keywords, in the same order and with no other words before or after. For example, an ad with the keyword "bagless vacuum" would only match searches with those exact words, not for a search such as "bagless vacuum cleaner".

Negative Match. Prevents searches containing this word being matched to your ad at all. This is very useful to prevent your ad being displayed in a context that's irrelevant: for example, you could have an ad with a broad match keyword of "vacuum" and a negative match keyword of "space". That way you'd eliminate people doing searches for "vacuum in space" who are probably more interested in the NASA site than your bagless vacuum cleaners!

Creating Landing Pages

When you created your ads you specified a "display URL" and a "destination URL". The display URL is shown in the ad, while the destination URL is where the user will actually be sent once they click the ad.

If you want your ads to be successful it is absolutely vital that the page you send visitors to is specifically tailored to meeting their exact need at the moment they clicked on the ad. Many AdWords beginners simply point their ads to the home page of their site, but that's almost always the wrong thing to do. If you've created an ad for a specific product and then simply dump visitors at your home page, how are they going to get the information they want? You can't expect them to then navigate through your site or use your site's search function to find the page they want. If you're advertising a product, have your AdWords ad take visitors directly to a page about exactly that product. Don't waste their time with a general introductory spiel or send them to a page that doesn't solve their problem. That just makes you look like you don't care about them.

A page that has been created specifically as a destination for an advertising campaign is called a "landing page", and it should be tuned to exactly match the hook or offer in your ad. It doesn't even have to be accessible through your normal website navigation: you may want to create a "hidden" page with information about a special offer, and then use an AdWords campaign to send people to that page directly.

Although it's not always necessary, a good objective is to have a separate landing page for every ad you run. That way you can tune the page to be a direct follow-on from the wording in your ads, providing potential customers with a seamless experience and an immediate indication that you're there to meet their needs.

Search Network vs Content Network

Earlier I explained that the search network refers to ads displayed alongside search results and matched to the user's search terms, while the content network refers to ads displayed on third party sites and matched to the page content. I recommended that you start your first ad campaign on just the search network and leave the content network alone initially.

Now that you have your first search network campaign underway it's time to start exploring the content network.

What you should keep in mind is that the behavior and mindset of people using the content network and the search network are very different and so your ads for the two networks need to be targeted differently.

If you think about the process of finding an answer to a question or solving an immediate problem, people who are using a search engine are in the early stages of seeking information while people viewing general websites are likely to be closer to finding an answer and having their immediate need satisfied. It may take a user only a few seconds to go from searching on keywords on a search engine to reading detailed information about their chosen topic on a website, but they go through a profound change of mindset in those few seconds and if you don't understand that change your ads will probably not be targeted effectively.

While they are using a search engine, users can be characterised as unsatisfied and focused on a specific question. Once they move from the search engine results to a general website they can be characterised as being more likely to be satisfied and therefore less focused and more open to other trains of thought.

Therefore people viewing your ad on the search network are actively searching for an answer to a specific question. That means they are less likely to be distracted by something that is peripheral to their immediate problem, but it also means that you can target your ad to meet their immediate need because you know what keywords they searched on. Ads on the search network therefore need to be very carefully tailored to address the immediate need of the user and should be as specific as possible to the search terms they have used or the problem they are trying to solve.

On the other hand, people who view your ads on the content network are more likely to have had their question answered and may be more receptive to advertising about other related issues.

Let me illustrate with a simple example.

Imagine you run a scuba training center in Maui and you want to reach out to potential customers who are planning to travel to the area on vacation. You can do this with two sets of ads, some on the search network and some on the content network. However, the ads need to be targeted and worded very differently.

On the search network you know that users are trying to answer a specific question, so it would make sense to target your search network ads for variations on the phrase "scuba training in Maui". Your service meets that immediate need and if someone is actively searching for that exact phrase you definitely want your ad to appear right where they will see it. They're a red-hot prospect and likely to be very receptive to ads that meet their need.

But going broader probably won't work. Sure, someone searching for "hotel in Maui" may be an ideal prospect, but they're focused on solving the immediate problem of finding a hotel and so they're less likely to care about ads for scuba diving right at that moment in time.

Once users reach the content network though it's a different story entirely. A user who searched for "hotel in Maui" and ended up on a hotel site or accommodation guide is further along the mental journey of solving their immediate problem, and so an ad for your scuba training services could be very successful on the content network when matched to keywords such as "Maui hotel", or "Maui whale watching" when those exact same keywords would be a total failure on the search network.

I strongly recommend that you run separate ad campaigns for the search and content networks. It will allow you not only to tune the ads much more accurately to match user requirements, but it will also allow you to break out the statistical reporting and track results across the networks independently.

Understanding Your Bills

Billing Frequency

At first it might seem that Google are billing you at odd times that don't make sense: sometimes it will be at 30 day intervals, sometimes sooner.

The reason is that Google do their billing based on both your credit history and your ad activity, and your credit history determines your credit limit. Simply put, you will be billed either when you reach your credit limit or at the end of your 30 day billing cycle – whichever comes first. Every time you are billed either because you reached your credit limit or because you reached the end of your billing cycle, the billing cycle is reset to 30 days from that date.

That way Google keep a safety net in place to minimise the risk of a runaway advertiser running up an enormous bill in a short time.

Credit Limits

When you first create your AdWords account you will have a default credit limit (often referred to in Google documentation as the "billing threshold") applied. In Australia the starting credit limit is AU$100, elsewhere it's US$50. If you never reach your limit it will never change: you'll simply be billed at the end of each billing cycle. However, every time you reach your limit before the end of the cycle your limit is raised to the next tier. In Australia the tiers are AU$100, then AU$250, then AU$500, then AU$1000. Elsewhere it's US$50, then US$200, then US$350, then US$500.

That might sound a bit confusing but it's actually a neat way to minimise the frequency with which big spenders are billed while simultaneously reducing the likelihood that a beginner will build up a huge bill unexpectedly. As you spend more your limit ratchets up over time to match.

Billing Summary Adjustments

Sometimes you may see strange "adjustment" entries in your Billing Summary.

Adjustments are generally one of two things: either a promotion or credit applied to your account; or what Google call an "overdelivery credit".

Overdelivery is a technique that Google use to try to ensure that you always get as many clicks as you are willing to pay for. Because it's impossible to exactly predict the popularity of specific keywords or ads the AdWords system builds in some padding and will often display your ad up to 20% more often than is actually necessary to achieve the number of click-throughs that you've paid for. You may therefore find for example that you've set a daily limit of say $20 with a CPC bid of $1, but due to Google's overdelivery policy there may have actually been 23 people who clicked your ad. This of course results in a bill for $23, exceeding your specified daily limit.

However, Google will do the right thing and never actually bill you for more than the limit you have set, so although in this scenario your Billing Summary would show that $23 of ads were purchased, a $3 overdelivery credit would also be automatically applied so your billing limit is not exceeded.

Conversely, on some occasions your ad may not achieve enough clicks to reach your limit and so you will only be billed for the actual number of clicks in that period. Overall your bill should only ever be less than or equal to your specified limit: never more.

Additional Resources

This quickstart guide is really just an introduction to AdWords. If you want to make the most of your online ad campaign I recommend you follow up with these resources.

Ultimate Guide To Google AdWords

If you want to really learn how to get the most out of it I highly recommend Perry Marshall and Bryan Todd's book. It's chock-full of information gleaned from years of experience creating and managing AdWords campaigns for a wide variety of clients.

www.perrymarshall.com/google/ultimateguide.htm

AdWords For Dummies

An excellent book from one of Perry Marshall's AdWords coaches, Howie Jacobson.

askhowie.com/book

How To Build A Website And Stay Sane

My business-oriented guide to developing a successful website. Aimed at the non-technical reader, it gives you the critical information you need to work productively with your web developer and create or redesign a website that will be a vital part of your business.

www.stay-sane.com

Inside AdWords Blog

A blog used by the Google AdWords product team: very useful if you want to keep track of all the latest changes.

adwords.blogspot.com

Direct links to these resources and more are provided online at:
www.adwords-quickstart.com/resources

> We altered the *blahblah* which improved our *blahblah* but the *blahblah* exceeded our *blahblah* so we hit the *blahblah* before the billing cycle ended

Glossary

Ad
An ad is the smallest definable unit in an AdWords campaign. It defines how the ad will appear to users and what URL they will go to when they click the ad.

Ad Group
An ad group is a mid-level collection of ads which share keywords and CPC bid value. Ad groups are created within campaigns.

Campaign
A campaign is a top-level grouping of ad groups with common attributes such as region and language targeting or product line. Each campaign can contain multiple ad groups.

Click Through
The act of clicking on an ad to visit the site being advertised.

Click Through Rate (CTR)
The percentage of people who see your ad and then click on it. For example, if your ad is displayed 1000 times and 34 people click on it your conversion rate is (34 / 1000) x 100, or 3.4%.

Conversion
A user performing some defined action in response to your ad. This could be a purchase, a newsletter signup, a report download, or some other activity depending on the objectives of your advertising campaign.

Conversion Rate
The percentage of people who click on your ad who then go on

to perform a conversion. For example, if 27 people click on your ad and then 12 of them download a report you are offering (your predefined conversion event) your conversion rate for that event is (12 / 27) x 100, or 44%.

Cost Per Click (CPC)

The amount that you pay to Google for each user who clicks on your ad. This can typically range from a few cents to a dollar or so, but can be much higher for hotly-contested keywords. This billing method is sometimes referred to as PPC, or "pay per click", as opposed to other ad billing methods such as CPM, or cost per thousand impressions.

Cost Per Thousand (CPM)

An alternative ad billing method where the advertiser pays per thousand ad impressions, irrespective of how many people click on the ad.

Destination URL

The web address to which users will be directed when they click on your ad.

Display URL

The web address to display in your ad. This is often an abbreviated version of the destination URL, such as the address of your homepage.

Impression

Your ad being displayed to a user, whether they click on it or not.

Keyword

A word or combination of words that users search on. AdWords ads can be targeted against specific keywords so that they only appear when those keywords are entered by a user.

Landing Page

A web page specifically designed as a site entry point for users responding to an advertising campaign.

Local Targeting

Limiting display of your ad to users in a specific geographic area such as a country, region, or city.

PageRank

A link-analysis algorithm used by Google to rate website quality and assign a quality score from 0 to 10. The term is also generally used to refer to the score itself. Often abbreviated simply "PR", particularly when referring to the score. For example, a well-ranked website could be said to have "PR 7".

Pay Per Click (PPC)

Another common term for Cost Per Click (CPC).

Placement Targeting

Running an ad campaign with ads configured to appear on specific nominated third-party websites.

Quality Score

A score assigned to ads by Google using a formula that factors in the click through rate, the relevance of ad text, the relevance of the advertiser's website, the historical performance of the selected keywords, and other metrics.

Search Engine Optimization (SEO)

Tuning a website to appear as high as possible in the search results when searching for specific keywords.

Thanks for reading!

I hope this little guide has been helpful in getting your AdWords marketing program underway.

I'd really love to hear your feedback about the book, so if you have a minute to spare I'd appreciate it if you could drop me an email at jon@oxer.com.au or submit the feedback form at www.adwords-quickstart.com/feedback.

And I'd be especially happy if you could submit a review and/or rating at your favorite online bookseller, such as Amazon.com or Barnes & Noble. The easiest way to do that is to follow the links from www.adwords-quickstart.com/buy and submit a review directly on the seller's site.

Thanks!

Jonathan

About The Author

Jonathan Oxer is founder and Technical Director of Internet Vision Technologies and is recognized as one of the pioneers of eBusiness.

His company was one of the first in the world to focus on managing commercial website content dynamically using databases. Since 1994 Jonathan and his staff have planned, implemented and managed websites, intranets, extranets, and custom web-based software for companies ranging from tiny backyard businesses to multinational corporations. You can learn more about his business, Internet Vision Technologies, at www.ivt.com.au.

Jonathan has presented conference papers, seminars, and tutorials on a wide variety of topics including software development, online marketing, eBusiness, and server management to thousands of people at conferences and companies around the world, and is a regular contributor to various newspapers and IT magazines. He has also been a guest speaker at Google headquarters in Mountain View, California on a number of occasions to deliver presentations on topics including virtual reality systems, hardware hacking, home automation, and software package management.

His other books include:

"How To Build A Website And Stay Sane" (Lulu, 2007)
www.stay-sane.com

"Ubuntu Hacks" (O'Reilly Media, 2006)
www.ubuntuhacks.com

Jonathan writes an irregular email newsletter called "Jon Oxer's eBusiness News". You can read past editions and subscribe free to receive future updates at www.stay-sane.com/ebusinessnews.

Jonathan's personal blog can be found at http://jon.oxer.com.au/.

Colophon

This book was prepared digitally using entirely Free / Open Source Software (FOSS). Writing and page layout were performed with OpenOffice.org running on Ubuntu Linux. Images were prepared with GIMP.

For more information on FOSS and the software used to prepare this book please visit:

    Linux Australia   www.linux.org.au/linux
    OpenOffice.org   www.openoffice.org
    Ubuntu Linux   www.ubuntu.org
    GIMP   www.gimp.org

www.ingramcontent.com/pod-product-compliance
Lightning Source LLC
Chambersburg PA
CBHW031536210526
45464CB00003B/1037